How Women Can Maximize Their Time and Increase Their Productivity

The Practical Guide to Overcome Procrastination and Get More Done in Less Time.

By MARIE A. NATOUX

REMA
WORDS THAT MATTER

v

Disclaimer

to be caused directly or indirectly by this book, nor do we make any claims or promises of your ability to generate income by using any of this information.

Table of Contents

PREFACE

"Don't be fooled by the calendar. There are only as many days in the year as you make use of. One man gets only a week's value out of a year while another man gets a full year's value out of a week."

-- Charles Richards

Have you ever wondered how some people may seem to have enough time to do whatever they want, whereas others are always rushing from task to task and never seem to finish anything? It's no gainsaying that we are enshrouded in lots of activities; managing time and events can be big to juggle, especially for working mothers. This is exactly why this book was written. It is centered on women, mostly working moms who want to combine career and womanhood responsibilities, through effective time management.

Time management is an art that needs to be mastered. It is an important modern skill that working women and moms need to cultivate and learn. It's a skill that is needed to harness opportunities. The mastery of time management will help stabilize your turbulent list of responsibilities. With this book, working mothers can rest assured to get information that will soothe their yearnings on how to effectively manage their time in order to skyrocket their efficiency and productivity.

I deeply believe in life principles and techniques 'do this and get that'. I had devoted my time to study and research successful working women's secrets, and I have shared a lot of techniques with you so you can be an organized employee and an envied mom for your family on a professional and personal level.

This book gives you the opportunity to learn the fundamentals and techniques of time management; What a to-do list can do for you, and how to create a successful one; how to balance personal life and career as a working woman; the techniques and habits of highly successful women; and how you can make decision on tasks based on the Urgent and Important Matrix. It was a pleasure for me to put all this information together to offer you a book that will make a significant impact on your life. I hope you enjoy it.

Introduction

"The best thing about the future is that it comes one day at a time."

\- Abraham Lincoln

Emphatically, women are natural homemakers, bond connectors, and every good ingredient that can make a home sweet and full of flavor. Nevertheless, we won't overlook the difficulties that surround all the nice features that make them stand out for time that hinges on urgency and pertinence.

As a working woman, you want to balance a lot of tasks together, and in that process, you multi-task which is not an effective way to maximize productivity. Time management is very crucial, and you need to understand and streamline the knowledge into your day to day activities. As you know when you say you are productive, it means you spawn and yield results.

This book will focus on how working women can balance personal, career and family catering together, with one not impeding the other. The question now is how can you use time management to track your progress, failures, and aspirations in life? Do you want to do yourself a favor? I will suggest you get a jotter and a pen to write down intricate meanings and values that you will soon absorb in this book. Have you done that? Then let's begin!

What should you look out for in this book as a reader?

1. This book will give a lucid road map for women to learn, imbibe, and achieve tasks within a short time and simultaneously being productive.

2. How women can plan their ample and jammed schedules to have a hitch-free day.

3. How to identify tasks that will bring excessive productivity rather than being slow down in the internment of perfectionism?

4. How to juggle our work under a constructive and analyzed time approach?

Based on the aims above, you should be excited concerning the prospect of this book, and I hope it will affect your lives positively. Let's get going!

CHAPTER ONE

Helping Women to Maximize Time and Reach Greater Peak and Productivity

"Time is more valuable than money. You can get more money, but you cannot get more time."

-- Jim Rohn

Time is a crucial parameter in everyone's life. It's a determinant of one's progress and failures. Time is very important, and if not used judiciously, it can be gone forever. In the modem world, it seems like we are working 24/7, but the question is "Is our investment in the time productive?" You can work round the clock, and your end product tends to show less than you put in. Time management is much more concerned with the efficacy of the end product and the utilization of a short time to create a big impact and outcome. It takes us to "What is Time Management?" Time management is the process of organizing, analyzing, planning, dividing your time between specific tasks or a range of activities. Time management helps us to be smart and not trying to impress them with hardness and endurance. Time management assuages stress that routine work tends to give, and if our stress is not managed, it could result in breakdown.

The 6 Major Benefits of Time Management

You might be asking why the learning of time management is important. It's really important to master the art of time management. Though it might be puzzling and difficult at first, you stand to rack up enormous benefits and ideas from Time management. Below are what you stand to gain:

1. Greater proficiency, efficiency, and productivity

Time management boosts your proficiency when it is on a high level. When you understand time management, you will know how to harness a short time to do some work and save large tasks until when you have a large block of time. For example, in your company, you are the head of the supervising and reporting unit. Untimely, your boss requests an impromptu report of a particular project in the next two hours, and during that period you have your thirty minutes recess. As someone who understands time management, you won't jump into writing the report, because you will be tensed. And there is a strong possibility you produce a shoddy report because you are not balanced, and you work under a stressed time frame. You can maximize your efficiency by using the thirty minutes recess to strategize on how the report will be, the format and all. You still have your two hours left because you've already planned everything during the recess. Now, you will move at the speed of light when filing your report. That is the art of time management. When you remember you have a list of work to do that could cause a high-stress level, but time management understanding will play a pivotal role to create a to-do list that will help you save energy and time.

2. Increased self-confidence

When you meet deadlines and your work is prompt, it increases your self-confidence. And trust me, you are on a wavy level. It feels awesome when you reflect on your day, and you were able to accomplish tasks. It gives you that joy and prospect to take new opportunities and connections.

3. Stress Mitigation

Stress is a reaction to excess pressure. It's normal to feel anxious when the workload is too heavy. You might ask yourself how you are going to finish all that work. This needless thinking could accumulate stress aside from the physical effort. Effective time management could give an inkling on resorting to what is called the To-do list. We will still expand on the to-do list later in the chapter. It is just a systematic way of planning and arranging events to clear space and fruitless time. In your to-do list, you set important tasks first; those that are a priority. For example, let's consider Mrs. Grace Benson tasks on Saturday:

- Garden watering and weed cutting

- washing and ironing of clothes
- cooking and cleaning utensils
- helping kids with assignment
- house cleaning and surroundings clearing
- fun time with family
- intimacy with husband
- watching a TV program
- buy groceries
- company's business proposal

Imagine one person faced with such a list of things to do? Won't she breakdown? Aside from the physical effort that requires strength, what about the mental aspect?

4. Increased opportunities

Time management can mold to become a trusted employee who submits quality gigs at stipulated deadlines. This will improve your personality on job ethics and provide you with a pathway to get better job opportunities. The efficacy of time management is boundless and endless.

5. Better results

Constantly not managing your time to specific tasks and projects can make your work less efficiently and short of effort. Time management helps you to prioritize your tasks by assigning bloc of time to a particular task so that you can have enough time to complete every project. Your quality work depends on the amount of time you sacrifice and not rushing to complete it ahead of a fast-approaching deadline.

6. Procrastination subdued

Firstly, you must understand that procrastination works against time management. Procrastination affects your function to concentrate in a motivated sense. I assume you are familiar with the term procrastination. It's a deadly mechanism that allows you to stay idle while killing you slowly on different ramifications. Time management will help block procrastination and improve your progression. For example, you have loads of work to do. You can use time management to divide the work, although you might not finish it. However, your planned schedule will salvage laziness and procrastination.

Here are 5 essentials tips on how to overcome procrastination and to increase your productivity.

6.1. Understand Procrastination: A problem highlighted is halfway to be solved. You should ask yourself why do you leave important assignments or work to the last minute? A better reflection from yourself may help you counter procrastination. According to research, procrastination can be psychological, and you can get help from a psychologist. It could simply be a bad habit, you have to take a stand against it.

6.2. Break up the work into smaller bits: As a mother, I am scared of voluminous work, and it helped my procrastination. Breaking assignments into smaller and simple tasks can help you get work done faster. Large chores do seem overwhelming and may cause postponement of tasks.

6.3. Recognize your procrastination activities: When you procrastinate, what do you engage in? Do you enjoy social platforms when you are supposed to do the company's sales summary? Analyze your activities and eliminate all distractions. You can freeze your social apps to block incoming messages.

6.4. Get others involved: Working moms can work with their family, friends, or co-workers to get tasks done. It's not bad when you collectively assign work. They will help you stop procrastination. Working with people can make you stay focused and bypass procrastination.

6.5. Stop the excuses: Working moms should be wary of making excuses every time. It derails work vibe and leads to procrastination. They should take responsibility. The common excuse working moms make is waiting for the perfect time to do a task. Such an excuse is unhealthy, and it moves you closer to procrastination.

6 Major Disadvantages of Poor Time Management

We can't bypass ineffective control of our time as it would always come to hurt us or make us feel down. Working moms should understand that ineffective time management can lead to complications. We shall enumerate some of the complications working mothers may face;

1. Poor Workflow

Improper time management can aggravate your workflow. The ability to be proactive is really important. Planning and sticking to your goals will help define your productivity and efficiency. I remember, one day, I woke up hurriedly after I realized I was late for work. I did wash the plates; I had to iron my clothes while doing that, I was making phone calls and preparing the kids for school. Unfortunately, my clothes got burnt, and I was totally out of control for that day. The problem is the workflow was much, and I hadn't planned to deal with it.

2. Wasted Time

Have you noticed when you don't have a plan for something you aiming, your day tends to be out of order? Yes, it happens very often. When you don't keep track of your events with stipulated time, you tend to use the day as it unfolds rather than what you planned to do. Time management ensures working moms don't have distractions and clutters that waste their precious time. When you have a schedule, you follow, and it's rare to just waste time on irrelevances and things that don't count. Time management helps you to use time judiciously by carefully analyzing, planning and dividing your duties. Some women engage in chit-chat when doing assignments, and it causes time-wasting and distraction.

3. Reduced work quality

I got a gig from one of my clients, and I supposed to start immediately due to the work complexity, but I was procrastinating. Eventually, the deadline caught up with me, and I did a shoddy job. I was very surprised when my client told me I didn't start the work early, and this is why the work content was obviously the outcome of a late rush. Poor time management makes your work quality suffer, and you tend to compromise the work standards.

4. Loss of control

Always keep in mind that you are the architect and designer of your home. You have to assume control of your events as a woman. You shouldn't be tossed to and fro by a lifeless task. Time management would ensure that. It's quite laughable that some women don't know what their next task is. This can result in mental battling and distress, which could lead to a high-stress level.

5. Poor reputation as a working mother

You need to be time conscious. If not, you will suffer a bad reputation for ineffective time management. If you can't be relied on to complete tasks for your client promptly, your reputation and your work ethic might be adversely affected. Time management will assuage you from losing jobs and also boost your confidence. It is instrumental in your day to day activities, career, home management, and other social events. Learning the techniques will help better your life as a whole and improve everything connected to you.

6. Missed Deadlines

If you don't organize your workload and set up a prioritized schedule, you will scramble to finish tasks at the last minute. Eventually, you will miss deadlines. Failing to meet expectations is bad for business. If clients can't count on you, they will take their business elsewhere. If you work for a company, missed deadlines might be cause for firing.

The 7 Basics of Time Management

Time management can be a puzzling skill to master. We all agree there is simply not enough time to manage all our activities and get everything done. When short on time, the most organized working mom can be stressed out. Imagine you manage a workload of tasks at home ranging from self-care to family care. And more you have your professional career to build. Connecting all these dots can be a herculean daily task. The strategies below will help you achieve your daily goals.

1. Plan ahead

Effective planning is the most important element of time management. Your planning should be in the form of a to-do list. Making a to-do list is not the problem but completing it can be somehow tricky. The key to finish the to-do list is by knowing yourself and know when you are most productive and alert. Your alertness level could be in the morning, or you are the type that hit stride at night. You just need to discover that to have the energy to complete your work. You're going to need a good planner. Your most challenging and important task should be saved for the period when your productivity level is high. Your to-do list should be in such that you take into account the amount of energy that will be expended on each task and put aside simpler and smaller tasks for times when you are less alert.

Good planning ahead will save you from nagging, frustration, and jammed day.

2. Set Priorities

Evaluation of tasks in order of priority is imperative. One of the commonest errors of time management is getting trampled in the form of distraction and procrastination. Time management is concerned about focus and concentration. How do busy moms balance tasks up when there is much to do? You don't have to be overwhelmed; setting priorities can make any workload seem doable even if you don't know you can. A lot of women want to be committed to their duties, but procrastination is like a poisonous chemical that disrupts their flow and gesture. You need to stand up against procrastination by taking a muse from Brain Tracy's book *Eat The Frog*. The frogs are those tasks you want to put off. Now imagine you complete the task; how would you feel? You feel accomplished, and every seemingly impossible task will be like a valley before you.

3. Stay focused on what you are doing

For example, you have a business presentation to do in the Executive board meeting. You don't want to give an insipid demonstration. You need to plan to strategize and impress your bosses. It is not the time you will be thinking about dinner or render help to kids for their assignments. You need to keep your mind glued to that particular presentation and not wandering to and fro. In that manner, you could lose track of consistency in your presenting arrangements and procedure. Task evaluation you need to work on should be the most important and urgent task and make that a top priority. Leave less important tasks or projects that haven't yet become urgent for later.

4. Avoid ineffective multitasking

Multitasking sounds pretty cool, but it's not effective towards productivity. A lot of working moms believe that time is maximized through multitasking. What they usually forget is that multitasking has shortcomings. It makes you feel you are making progress doing two things at a time, but in reality, you tend to begin the two tasks at a time, and you end up not completing them. For instance, you are ironing clothes, and at the same time attending to your wards, you know how kids can frustrate one to the point you forgot you were ironing, and you might end up burning your clothes. Multitask is thereby not effective. The best way to manage your time is to focus on a single task at a time and give it your full attention to avoid error and disconnection.

5. Eliminate distraction

I do tell people that distraction is all around us, and it is unavoidable so to say. Distraction is one of the most productivity killers and could be in any form, depending on anything that is obstructing your progress. For example, coworkers can affect your speed on work completion; smartphone and social platforms can take a huge chunk of your time if you don't control it. According to a study by Think Money, a third of employees are distracted for as much as three hours of the workday. If you, as a mother, enjoy distraction, then it is time to eliminate it. Although it may take a while to adjust, you can always do it if you set your mind on it. For instance, you are always busy with your smartphone playing; as you are doing so, you are checking your social media platforms. How can you minimize that? You can leave your smartphone locked in a desk drawer during the day, or use freezing apps that will block notifications and messages popping in.

6. Segregate work and motherhood responsibilities

Professional work and parental responsibilities are two different things and should not be mixed. One of the secrets of time management is sticking to where your capacity is needed. For example, when you are working, let your full attention be on your work and avoid divided minds. When you get home, put your mom hat on and leave job responsibilities at the office. You just have to be mindful of your responsibilities. For instance, you are a teacher, and it requires to take homework like you want to grade papers. You should do that when your kids are off to bed. There has to be an end to your day. As the saying goes Practice makes perfection. Management of time and energy comes with practice. When you practice time management often, you will get better with your accomplishments.

7. Reward yourself for good work

A great motivator for good time management is a reward. No reward is too small or too big. You don't have to buy heaven and earth because you want to reward yourself. You can decide to go for a night walk with a juicy wine to reflect on the tactics used and trust me, you will smile and feel gushy. Rewards keep you motivated on the job and can help you achieve a better work-life balance.

Conclusively, I presume you understand the basis of time management, and this will help further your learning. The next aspect to be dealt with is how to set up a to-do list and tips to decode while setting up one. Are you ready for the next action? Let's begin!

CHAPTER TWO

The 80/20 Rule and How It Can Help You Increase Your Productivity

"One reason so few of us achieve what we truly want is that we never direct our focus; we never concentrate our power. Most people dabble their way through life, never deciding to master anything in particular."

--Tony Robbins.

As a working woman, it is fundamental for you to have a clear understanding of what the 80/20 rule is. Also called the Pareto principle, it is quite easy to follow, but only if you devote yourself to it. But first, what does it really mean? To keep it short, let's say that 80% of what we do is pointless. Only 20% of our efforts yield 80% of the results. The idea is that 80% of our output comes from 20% of our efforts. That is a simple way to make you realize that the majority of your results - the 80% - come from a minority of your inputs -the 20%. What is trick is to figure out the most important 20% of your tasks.

To make it easier for you: consider that you have ten tasks to perform for the whole week. You have to figure out the two tasks which are the most important for you and will make up for the other eight tasks. Because these two tasks might be long, tough, and challenging, you will be expected to spend most time on them. Many are trapped in the 80% low-value tasks, only to avoid the 20% long and challenging tasks that can bring 80% of results. Those people who appear to be busy all day long but seem to accomplish very little. This is always because they are busy working on tasks that are of low value while they are procrastinating on one or two activities that could make a real difference. The most valuable tasks you can do each day are often the hardest and most complex, but the payoff and rewards for completing them can be tremendous.

That being said, every time you start your work, you better ask yourself if what you're going to do is the important 20% of your tasks that will put you in a much better position instead of doing the other small tasks. You have to eat the frog, just to paraphrase Brian Tracy in his book *Eat the Frog*.

The rule for this is: resist the temptation to clear up small things first. If you choose to start your day working on low-value tasks, you will soon develop the habit of always starting and working on low-value tasks.

You can examine your frustrations and issues using the Pareto Principle if you ask these two questions:

- Which 20% of your current efforts are resulting in 80% of your desired outcomes and happiness?
- Which 20% of your current efforts are causing 80% of your problems and unhappiness?

Don't just guess! Instead, create a specific time schedule to get an overview of how you actually spend your time in an average working week.

Remember, nothing ever comes easy; so doesn't time management. If you want to bring a positive change in your life, you've got to make the 80/20 rule an integral part of your life, especially in the creation of your daily to-do lists.

Effective To-Do List: A Powerful Secret Weapon

In the previous chapter, we made a glint reference of how to tap the goodies embedded in making a to-do list for our tasks. This chapter will elaborate on tips for setting up an effective to-do list. Basically, a to-do list simply contains tasks you need to get done on a given day. Your to-do list is like a mechanism that helps you manage your life, prioritize tasks, and take you closer to your accomplishments. The overall purpose of creating a to-do list is to remember tasks and create a plan of action to accomplish them.

The to-do list is known to be personal. However, you can also create a to-do list for general-purposes like big projects. Longer to-do lists can help break a larger chunk of tasks to smaller units and help you visualize the necessary steps you can take to achieve it. The next question on your mind would be Why learn how to use it? Learning how to use a to-do list will help you do two specific things: improve how you manage your time and reduce stress levels.

1. Improve how you manage your Time

A to-do list will help you to be time conscious. You won't do tasks haphazardly. It will create a clear road map for your task, and your time coordinate will kick off from there. When you compose and organize your to-do list, you will observe the most important, and you will apportion time;

the less important can be squeezed to balance things up. For example, you have a business lunch near a store; you want to pick up goods. You can do the two tasks on a run, like using a stone to kill two birds.

2. Organization reduces stress

Stress can be energy-draining, and if it's accumulated much in the body, it can cause body breakdown. A disorganized person is a stressed person. Your to-do list will help you coordinate your energy on something that worth it and not crashing anything that comes your way. Organizing your to-do list can reduce stress in three ways;

> **2.1. Reducing forgetfulness.** -Trust me, a task written down is better than random brain selection. You tend to be direct and not wandering around in the midst of task abundance. For example, you write tasks to be done on your to-do list; you're less likely to forget about them, and it is registered in your subconscious.

> **2.2. Breaking tasks down.** -The to-do list helps you define your task. Have you ever been engrossed in your activities, and you are like how will I start? But when you make a to-do list, you will see the task in a much simpler manner, and you can have the confidence to mount a challenge on the task. Breaking tasks down also enables you to more

effectively and easily plan and set intermittent deadlines to ensure that you complete everything in time.

2.3. Productivity level increased. -You can increase your productivity level with a to-do list. Have you ever felt accomplished just mere writing your tasks down? it seems you have done it psychologically, and this will boost your motivation level, and before you know it, you already did it.

I hope you can see why you really need to start using a to-do list. Aside from its versatility, its simplicity can't be overstressed.

10 Tips on How to Set Up a To-Do List to Skyrocket Your Productivity and Efficiency Level.

Career, raising kids, work obligations, hangouts with friends, marriage commitment, achieving goals, and making deadlines seem harder than we think. Creating a to-do list can make a seemingly impossible task possible, maximize your productivity level depending on your input, and help you reach your larger goals.

I have highlighted 10 tips to help you organize your life into a manageable list. Take each step one after the other. Making a to-do list is really a personal decision, and most of us who believe in the power of to-do lists might not know how to create a successful one, but relax, I will help you with a step by step guide to creating a working to-do list for yourself.

1. Pick a medium

Your to-do list can be in any form and size, depending on what you want. But writing it on a sheet of paper is the worst thing you can do; it's ineffective and could be lost. Being in a tech-friendly century where digital apps are around us, using technology to set up a to-do list is a much better idea. There are fascinating apps that will help you set up a to-do list with ease. The stress of creating or formatting your to-do list can be time-wasting and energy-consuming.

2. Make multiple list

There is no limit to your to-do list creation. You can have a master to-do list that will contain all you want to do. For example, the master to-do list can have tasks you want to do in the long run, like sign up for an online course, daily savings of a certain amount of money, clean your house and all. You can create another to-do list for activities you want to do in the next seven days. The third list can be a HIT (High impact tasks) that you will do immediately or for the day like phone calls, laundry, finish work presentation, etc. You should refer to the master list and the second list every day to check the one that will move to the HIT list. You are going to make quick progress if you use that tactic.

3. Prioritize, Prioritize, Prioritize

Working women need to prioritize the most difficult tasks. All tasks aren't the same. In the economy, there is something called 'opportunity cost'. Basically, it means that you have to identify the cost of each task, their relevancy, and if it is possible to forgo for now and do it later. You need to apply such a tactic. Do the MITs (Most important tasks) first; don't fall in the pit of ticking off easy tasks ASAP in the name of feeling accomplished while leaving more difficult ones for later. You could be less productive with that tactic instead of kick-off you with at least two activities that need to get done absolutely today. The beauty of that idea is that even if you don't get to finish, you will be feeling accomplished doing the most important tasks. After all, productivity has been enhanced.

4. Break it down

There is always this fear factor when the task appears to be very big. It seems you want to work on a mountain and the task seems impossible, but when you break it down, it is nothing much to handle. Maybe you want to work on a research paper. In the real sense, that kind of work is tedious, and it needs analyzing and research. Your to-do list will help you divide it into units doable. You can start by breaking the research work into chapters. Pick each chapter daily and appoint a specific time to work on it. When you do that, the mountain becomes plain.

5. Stay specific

Your to-do list should be specific. It should be a physical action, something that can be done in one sitting. Although there is a bigger to-do list that involves shared work and interest with others, that is general work, and it will require lots of time. You can save yourself the stress of working at a low pace with others by writing your necessary steps and roles need to play.

6. Timing

You don't just create a to-do list that has no timing limit for schedule and others, it will make you sloppy and time expended. You need to put a time estimate for each item so you can speed up your work. It can even make the to-do-list more colorful when you add places or locations and time together. For example, Laundry 4-6 p.m. at Crest Ford; clean out inbox 6-7 p.m. at Star rock; when time is up, it's up.

7. Make it public

When I say public, I don't mean you are going about telling everyone you've made a to-do list. As a working woman, you need to be accountable for your actions, and when you know what accountability really entails, it will help you to be productive with your decisions. It might seem awkward, but the best way to be accountable is when someone watches over you. One of the ways to do that is to talk about it with a relative or a close friend. Why should you do this? It will help keep you in check and be a laughing stock if you don't complete your task, and this will help your productivity because you want to impress people who are watching you.

8. Encourage yourself

Encouragement is a powerful tool that can boost your productivity level as a woman. You need to remind yourself how great you were the last time you completed your task, and how great you will become if you could complete this one. This will increase your productivity at an exponential level. Write down your accomplishments no matter how small it is.

9. Start fresh

Some to-do lists are clogged with colorful highlighters and yet undone or partially done. You need to make your to-do list fresh and remove old items that were supposed to be done. Make a new list every day, so the same old items don't cloud your agenda.

10. Be flexible

You need to be flexible with your approach towards your to-do list in case of emergency or unplanned contingency shows up. Always leave about 10 to 15 minutes of cushion time in between items on the to-do list in case something pops up (say your kid collapse or the computer crashes). If any glitch happens, just stay relaxed and breathe. At least you've accomplished one MIT in a day; the rest will be taken care of later. Such things happen, and we must understand that uncertainty is a factor of productivity. So, as a working woman, you need to be proactive and flexible in your dealings.

Conclusively, the highlighted tips above have helped you understand the efficacy of the to-do list, and how it can help you maximize dissipated time, enhanced efficiency, and productivity maximization. The journey of time management has been interesting so far. It will get more interesting as we unfold deeper information. Are you ready for the next chapter? Stay relaxed!

CHAPTER THREE

How Women Can Handle Professional and Personal Life?

"Determine never to be idle. No person will have occasion to complain of the want of time who never loses any. It is wonderful how much can be done if we are always doing."

- Thomas Jefferson

Women are not limiting their exploration. They want to go beyond being a supportive wife, gentle, caring, and responsible mother. They also want to enjoy their career, being financially independent, enjoy good nights of sleep, and having fun. It's possible to get all, having a good family and a thriving career. Laura Vanderkam said "People seem to have this idea that having a full-time job leaves no space for many other things, but clearly that's not true. It is quite possible to have a more than a full-time job and have a very full personal life, too. It's just a matter of where that time goes."

For working women, every day seems daunting, and you must know that being a working mom goes beyond domestic chores and work responsibilities. This is why time management for working moms is pivotal. Time management techniques will help them to combat distractions and overwhelming issues. Most women struggle to strike the right work-life balance and post-marriage era. But as they say, resilience is one of the greatest strengths of a woman. With the right techniques, you can always be on top of your responsibilities. I will highlight essential and proved techniques that will help strengthen you in spite of the struggles.

1. Toughest tasks plan early in the morning

Rising early to plan your day can be the perfect time to know how your day will be. Early morning rise tends to make your brain feel relaxed, sharper, and alert. During that time, you are less distracted. This practice will help you plan your day and manage your priorities. To facilitate your thinking, you can take a little walk and meditate. It will help you feel relaxed and think straight. A case study by Vanderkam and his colleagues shows that our energy level is increased in the morning by 8 am. As a working mom, take advantage of early rising to plan and have a hitch-free day.

2. Sort out your priorities

Knowing your priorities as a working woman is important. You don't want to do a task that is not boosting your productivity. You want to be a successful working woman who has order priorities both professionally and personally. How do you set your properties right? You need to ask yourself some questions like "What can't be compromised or is completely non-negotiable? What are the most-important commitments at work and family?" Answers to these questions will help you make decisions and adjustments.

3. Be accountable to your profession

Accountability makes you more committed to your course and goals in life. As a working woman, you need to be accountable for your profession. Don't live a life of "I don't care." Usually, working women make the mistake of mixing concerns. At your workplace, forget your home concerns and problems. Be focused on your work, and you will get the respect of other colleagues as a professional. Do not let anyone down, and don't let anyone doubt your working capabilities. During recess, you can check up on home, make calls to friends and family. Itemizing each need differently will make you professionally accountable.

4. Talk it out with your employers

As a working woman, keep communication flow and open. Interact with your boss, HR, supervisors, etc. Cultivate a transparent and honest habit in your workplace. For instance, you are stuck in traffic while taking your kids to school, make a call to the appropriate department to explain the delay, and if it is going to be a problem, then come up with alternatives so that one side of your responsibility won't affect another. Your productivity is really important.

5. Avoid procrastination

We've talked more about procrastination in the previous chapter. It shows how procrastination can be a deadly stumbling block to your productivity and success. If you don't curb procrastination, it could become a repulsive habit. Putting off tasks for another time hampers the time management process. Completing tasks at the dead time is most stressful because the task will be devoid of meaning and time management planning. Working Women should not procrastinate. I understand sometimes tiredness might take its toll on you, but you can always take the first step which is 'start it'. Working women should also avoid doing less important tasks at the expense of the important ones, which may consequently be worse later.

6. Delegate and start saying No

The art of delegation teaches you to be in control of your life. Most working moms seem to be tossed by the wind of tasks. I don't understand why some of them always want to act like they can do all, and in the real sense, they are struggling. No is as simple as Yes. Learn to say No if you don't have the time and strength to perform a task. Acknowledgment of helpless situation can help ease the enormous workload of your shoulder.

By doing everything yourself, you are only putting excessive pressure on your body, and the result could be a breakdown in the future. At times, a need may arise from a co-worker asking you to help with a particular project. And you as well still have a lot you are struggling with, and you accept to help just to be a good and hardworking colleague; you only expose yourself and time organization messed up.

It's best to decide what you can do and what others can do. Seek help from co-workers, spouses, and family members. If you want to enjoy productivity at the highest level, cultivate the habit of saying 'No' when it is needed and learn the art of delegation. A case study below will help you understand better.

Case Study:

"Jenny was the leader of a busy, highly reactive team, with constant and urgent demands on her time. She knew that she needed to spend some time thinking through the implementation of a particular policy, but it was very hard to set aside the time.

In a development discussion, Sara, one of her team members, expressed her desire to do some more strategic work to build up her skills. Jenny saw an opportunity for both of them and offered Sara the opportunity to prepare the initial paper on implementing the policy.

Sara jumped at the chance and produced an excellent, well-thought-through paper which was a great foundation for further work."

The case study above shows how working mothers can use delegating skills to save time for themselves and also enjoy shared success with the doer. We must understand when to say No blatantly and when to delegate the task to someone else to reduce too much workload for yourself.

7. Stay connected during the day

As long as you want to keep distractions away, you still have to enjoy your social life to some extent. You can have a balanced social life with your career. It depends on how you manage your time. Thanks to technology, it is closer to us than ever before. You can use it to monitor the well beings of your loved ones, no matter how busy you seem to be. Working mothers can easily stay connected to their children and friends while working in the office, via social platforms like Facebook, WhatsApp, and other networks. Maybe you miss your kid, you can do video calls; you seem joyful and at the other end, the child feels relaxed that his mom is always near no matter the hours she works.

8. Optimism is the key to all

Optimism is the key that will unlock your potentials. It will help your demotivation and underestimation when you delegated work or said No due to your time management plans. Women face lots of challenges ranging from home issues to work glitch which could be stressful, and heads bow down. But take solace in optimism, it will give you the confidence and be prospectus at home and work.

9. Limit distractions and time-wasters

You can't run from your shadow, so it is for distractions. We are circulated with distractions and avoiding all these distractions is not really possible but can be reduced. Every minute is crucial as a working mum both home and office. If you calculate the time of distraction some people expended daily it is nothing less than 3 hours per day. If you want to be productive you need to keep gossip workers, Internet surfers, and smartphones at bay. Set a specific time to check mails for review and approval and when you get home don't spend all the time on TV but use it to You can't run from your shadow, so it is for distractions. We are circulated with distractions and avoiding all these distractions is not really possible but can be reduced.

Every minute is crucial as a working mom, both at home and office. If you calculate the time of distraction some people expended daily, it is nothing less than 3 hours per day. If you want to be productive you need to keep gossip workers, Internet surfers, and smartphones at bay. Set a specific time to check mails for review and approval. And when you get home don't spend all the time on TV. Use it instead to strengthen the bond with your kids and spouse.

10. Make some time for yourself

Healthwise, it's not appropriate to work all through the day without having proper rest and enjoyment mood. The secret to maintaining an ideal work-life balance is to enjoy yourself and do things you love. Spoil yourself, you deserve pampering as a working mom. It's not easy. Go to the spa to have a massage, go to the beach to enjoy nature with family, and if you haven't had sexual experience for a long time, use that period to explore sex adventure. The summary is that when you are in good shape, that's when you can cater to your family. As you work, don't forget to have fun.

We've come to the end of time management techniques. I would love to share successful working women's habits with you. Are you ready? Let's get started!

Time Management Habits of Successful Women

The first part of your game as a working mom might be employed, and the second part is to be successful in your career. It simply means you have to work hard simultaneously to achieve good results. Unfortunately, we neglect the main reason why most working moms fail. All is how they take one vital thing very lightly and that is their time. The importance of time management can't be stressed. It is imperative for working moms to have time management skills at their disposal.

Time management is herculean for women unlike men as studies reveal that the percentage of women is high as compared to men. The reason is due to domestic work and career work unbalanced. If you are facing that problem as a working mom, then this book will liberate you with proven habits that you will need to follow to get success in your professional life, without sabotaging your personal life.

- Don't follow multitudes, plan and be unique.
- Set priority limit
- Create time for social activities like family, social platforms, personal development, and stick to it.
- Make your morning profitable
- Be an early riser
- Categorize your time

- Be flexible with your approach and be proactive
- Maintain discipline

Conclusively, working mothers should be prepared to sacrifice and make adjustments to ensure an ideal life-work balance. To enjoy the pleasure of being a house manager and professional in your work, then you need to prioritize your time, and you will celebrate your life from work to being a great mother.

CHAPTER FOUR

The Eisenhower Matrix: How to Make Decisions on Urgent and Important Tasks?

"Most of us spend too much time on what is urgent, and not enough time on what is important."

-- Steven Covey

After a whole day, do you sometimes feel you can't point to something serious you've done? Do you sometimes feel like you are managing problems all the time? If yes, it definitely means you are confusing the important with the urgent.

Most working women are stuck in that dilemma, and sometimes if not managed well, that can cause serious stress. This chapter will explore the Urgency vs Importance model, and how it can help you make quick decisions on tasks.

An Urgent/Important matrix helps to review your task base on some considerations like "which one is important that will contribute to your growth, goals, and target; and which are essentially unknown distractions."

We will use the Urgent / Important matrix to determine how your time can be judiciously used. Time management is about efficiency and productivity. If you want to make headway, you need to know the important task that will contribute to your goals. To understand the two determinants, let's explain each on a broader level.

Urgent: it simply means the task demands immediate attention. These are the task that comes with the sound of 'Now'. Urgent tasks position you in a reactive situation, and it affects your organization. Usually, at work, urgent tasks contribute to help someone else's goal rather than yours.

Important:

On a personal and professional level, these are activities that help reach your goal and outcome. They contribute to long term plans, missions, goals, and vision. An important task could be urgent, but your mode of reaction to it is always responsive, which gives rise to rational thinking and open to new opportunities while remaining calm and not under the command of 'Now'.

Most working women fall into the trap that urgent activities are also important, and this is because it demands immediate attention. We will not shy from the fact that a lot has hampered us to give more attention to pressing things, which are just short moments in terms of lasting impact.

Thanks to Urgency/Important Matrix created by former US president Eisenhower and Stephen Covey. "What is important is seldom urgent and what is urgent is seldom important, sums up the concept perfectly."

The Eisenhower principle is a smart and simple tool that can be used to gauge productivity level as you respond to the two determinant factors. It helps you determine the most important task rather than the urgent, which is driven by natural affinity towards urgency. To understand the urgent and important matrix, we will divide it into quadrants for better understanding.

Quadrant 1: Urgent and Important Tasks:

In this quadrant, the task is urgent and also important. The task here is marked with crisis, problems, and deadlines. The urgent and important task is of two distinct types: the unforeseen and the one you've left to the last minute. Last-minute tasks can be averted by avoiding procrastination through planning.

We can't see crises and problems. They are unforeseen, but we can make our schedule to be proactive in setting up to accommodate unplanned contingency. You need to be proactive in your dealings when you have lots of urgent and important tasks. You can detect the foreseen crisis and quickly schedule to prioritize or eliminated so that urgent task doesn't become important every time.

Examples of Urgent and important tasks.

- Certain emails (That could be a job offer or an email for a new business opportunity that requires immediate action, etc.)
- Term paper deadline
- Tax deadline
- Wife in the emergency room
- Car engine spoilt
- Household chores
- You have a heart attack and end up in the hospital
- You get a call from your kid principal saying you need to come in for a meeting about his behavior.

The examples above show some crises are foreseen and other unforeseen. With a bit of planning, some of the examples could be done outright or eliminated. You can pay your tax in advance to when it is due to avoid late hour rush, also your term paper can be scheduled so you work ahead of time.

Urgent and important tasks can't be eliminated, but they can be reduced through your proactivity and sensitivity.

Quadrant 2: Not Urgent but Important Tasks

These are activities you need to concentrate your energy on because it defines your goal achievement. Time management is needed here to help you do it properly, so they don't turn to urgent tasks. This quadrant is concerned with strengthening relationships, future projects, and improving yourself.

Here are some specific examples of Not Urgent but Important Tasks:

- Day planning
- Weekly planning
- Long-term planning
- Exercising
- Spending time with Family
- Reading books
- Taking online class
- Spending time with a rewarding hobby
- Studying
- Meditating
- Religious programs
- Car and home maintenance
- Date night with your spouse.
- Creating a budget and savings plan etc.

You should invest your time in Quadrant Two. It provides you with self-satisfaction, happiness, and success. It's sad that people still have difficulty with Quadrant two, and it is due to two reasons:

1. You don't know what's truly important to you. - If you don't know the value of what matters to you, you will just expend your time on things that do not affect you positively.

2. Present bias. - We have a natural tendency to pressing concerns than important concerns. You won't be motivated to do something if there is no deadline looming, and it affects a large number of working moms. We tend to bow to urgency than something that possess core values.

Most of the time, you don't do Quadrant two tasks because they are not pressing. Living your lives intentionally and proactively can help you overcome the inherent bias towards Quadrant two. You just have to decide radically that you are going to do it.

Quadrant 3: Urgent and Not Important Tasks

These activities don't affect your goals. They are urgent but not important, and they are not building any long-term plan, opportunities, or vision. You ask yourself "do these activities need to be done?" If yes, can they be rescheduled?

It is polite to just say No because most activities in Quadrant three are interruptions from other people. You are helping them fulfill their own goals and resolve their problems.

Below are examples of Quadrant three activities:

- Chatting
- Phone calls
- Text messages
- Most emails (some emails could be urgent and important)
- A co-worker who comes by your desk during your prime working time to ask a favor.
- Request from a former employee to write a letter of recommendation on his behalf (it's probably important to him, but let's face it, it's probably not that important to you)
- Mom drops in unannounced and wants your help with a chore

You can see these are urgent tasks, but you aren't affected positively. You only fulfill others' desires and you should not invest much energy here. It will slow down your productivity.

Quadrant 4: Not Urgent and Not Important Tasks

The activities here are neither important nor urgent. They are primarily distractions and should be outright avoided. These are activities that you can cancel or ignore politely by saying 'No' and explain why. Your productivity is really important, and if anything is not racking up for your desired outcome, just keep it off.

Below are examples of Quadrant Four:
- Watching TV
- Surfing the web
- Playing video games
- Scrolling through Facebook, Twitter, Instagram
- Shopping spree
- Excessive chatting

Most working women have found themselves in the Quadrant four, or should I say most people generally are in that Quadrant four. Well, I don't say you should not enjoy Quadrant four but make it minimal. Don't make it your important and urgent task because it will slow down your productivity and merely time-wasting.

As you can see, Urgent/Important Matrix will help you make more commitment to the most important task, and not a reactive pressing needs and adjustment to where it is necessary. Urgent/Important Matrix will help your efficiency and productivity level. it is a simple tool but effective one for prioritizing your to-do list based on the level of urgency and importance of each task.

Here is what you need to remember:

	URGENT	NOT URGENT
IMPORTANT	**1** **DO**	**2** **PLAN**
NOT IMPORTANT	**3** **DELEGATE**	**4** **ELIMINATE**

CHAPTER FIVE

How to Get More Done in Less Time as a Stay-At-Home Mom?

" I think it's a tough road if you're a stay-at-home mom, a working mom, if you have a partner, if you don't. It's the best job in the world, and the toughest job in the world all at the same time."

--Angela Kinsey

The maintenance, tending to family affairs, and upkeep of a home can be very herculean and stressful for housewives. You can be a housewife and still progress your career while managing home affairs.

I remember when I started my blogging career, it wasn't easy at the start, and I was choked with excessive home clutters but with the help of some time management plans, I scaled through. There is a notion that housewives enjoy because they don't have where to go, they are always at home; it's even harder to be in a sedentary state. There is a joy that comes with mobility when you work outside than staying in your home and do the same thing every day. Have you ever had a whole lot of time to do house chores and taking care of the kids, but you never seem to finish it? It always seems as if time has grown wings, Alas, 24 hours are gone, and you still have a whole lot of things you have not done from yesterday. You are stuck among the following duties like waking up early to cook, house chores, the kids and having personal time No wonder those wrinkles on your face keep increasing!

Sometimes you wonder how you spent your time, and how time seemed to fly every day even though everyone thought you had a lot of time since you do stay at home - as a wife and mother. As someone who had been through this before, I would confidently tell you that you are not the only one in this struggle and it all boils down to "TIME MANAGEMENT".

Time management is one skill that cannot be overemphasized in your everyday life and especially as a housewife, it is one skill that could make you more confident and organized in everything you do. Below are the practical steps I used:

1. Self-Appraisal:

I know this may seem like a joke to you, the question that pops on your mind is "What does self-appraisal has to do with time management?" I tell you, it has a whole lot to do. When you appreciate yourself more for the things you have done, it becomes relatively easier to do the other tasks faster mentally. You appreciate yourself for washing a full basket of clothes, it will give you ginger to wash the dishes without complaint. We know as women, we love praises, so complimenting yourself is the first step to help you manage your time so that you can deliver your duties giddily.

I would give you a few tips through which you can appreciate yourself time-wise and work-wise. There you go:

A. Every time you clean the kitchen on schedule, give yourself a warm bath to reward yourself. When you do this, you find it easier and faster to clean the kitchen since you are thinking of that warm bath waiting for you. You know what they say," The reward could stop but habits never die."

B. Always remind yourself that being a housewife is a super cool thing. Having the right mindset can help you do your job 10 times faster because you are happier doing it. These might seem like it has no relationship with managing your time well, but I discovered that when I became a happier housewife. I did the chores with more speed and accuracy.

2. Early Rise

Now, that you appreciate yourself more, the next to do is to cultivate early rising. I know this might seem like what you do every time, but it's really not. For me, waking up early would mean waking up 30- 45 minutes earlier than usual to think about my plans for the day, what I would love to do first, the food, the dishes, etc. Sometimes, waking up early could mean sitting quietly on your bed and doing nothing, just nothing! Think about your plans for the day, set your schedules within that time, the most important thing to the least important. That time is to plan for the day or sitting down to reflect.

3. Plan

Yes, I have got to that part where you are frowning your face and thinking of what exactly to plan for, but you forgot that who doesn't plan has planned to fail. You need to plan for the day. You start from the most important things you need to do to the least important thing so that even if you don't finish, you get at least your major priorities done before the end of the day. The plan also helps you not miss important things out, and at the end of the day, you realize you managed your time well just because of a little plan. It does seem funny right? But dear mom, you absolutely need to have a plan and don't forget to plan it.

It is very important to set timers for your plans. The time! In every plan, you have to have a stipulated amount of time to execute it. You have about 12 hours in the day and believe me when I tell you that a plan without a timer is no plan. You have got to set that 30 minutes you need to cook, you have to set that time you need to clean, it is all about self-discipline. Time management is all about discipline too. You have to discipline yourself to be time conscious.

4. Stick to the time and plans

Now that you have a plan, and timers have been set, you need to stick to your time. It is one thing that helps a lot in managing your time well. If the time stipulated for cleaning the dishes is 1 hour, try as much as possible to use a maximum of that time and nothing more. It might seem harder at first but then, practice makes perfect. I discover that anytime I follow my time and plan effectively, I get to do a whole lot more in my plan, and at the end of the day, I feel accomplished. And let me tell you something quietly, it helps the sex too because a happy woman is a sexier woman! Now, this is also the point where I would review the part on self-appraisal, if you do some of the chores within the slated time, reward yourself! You could take that ice cream you always wanted; it might just be the drive to be faster the next day!

5. Make Realistic Plans

The honest but bitter truth is that your plans won't always be perfect. You won't always do all that's in your plans, that's why there is room for spillovers. But, the most important thing at this stage is making realistic plans, don't make plans you know you can never fulfill, don't plan to clean the house in 30 minutes when you know an hour is not even enough to complete the task, you need to know that it's not about how much you have done, but how well you have done. Make your plans realistic, don't make "castles in the air" plans!

6. Beware of negative impact of Social Media

Have you ever been on Facebook just to post a picture and like your husband's latest post, and you end up spending the whole day on Facebook? Have you ever put some food on the fire and checked a few posts on Twitter and the food got burnt? I am sure you wondered how many minutes you spent liking a few posts just like I did. Alas, mine wasn't funny. I almost burnt the kitchen because I needed to check a news feed on Facebook.

I have discovered that while we are on social media, we spend a lot of time going from one post to another when all we went there to do is like a few posts. Well for me, the discipline here is that I don't even go near my social media accounts while working because they could disrupt the plans I have for the whole day. Checking a message on my email could direct me to google and distract me. When you are working, be disciplined enough to never go on social media. Why don't you finish that work and reward yourself with a nice social media time? This could help you stick to time because a whole lot of time we make plans which we never follow.

7. Don't Procrastinate

I know this is a habit that most people find hard to let go, but dear wife/mother, to manage your time effectively, you need to stop procrastinating. I tell you, procrastination is like cancer, it spreads until you cancel all your plans. You need to remember that each day has its own plans, and spillovers from the last day could disrupt the following day plans. Why don't you just lay that bed now and not wait till tomorrow? Stop giving excuses not to do the work right away, break it into smaller pieces if it would help, take mini breaks if it would help. Procrastination stops you from feeling accomplished at the end of the day and prevents you from managing your time faster.

8. Learn to say NO

The ability to say NO is one thing that helps in managing your time well, even though it may seem unrelated. Saying no to some external demands when they can't seem to work with your plans could help you a whole lot. No matter how hard it is to say NO, saying it when needed could help you avoid a cluster of tasks you really shouldn't be involved in. If you realize going to the supermarket on Saturday isn't as feasible as going on Wednesday, you need to say NO to shopping on Saturdays then. You don't have to always say YES to every task because you seem to always be home, say NO when it doesn't seem to work with your plans. This could help you in managing time well, not only as housewives but also as an individual.

9. Be Flexible

You also need to make your plans flexible and not rigid. No one wants to do the same thing every day. Your routine should be very flexible so as to decrease the chance of boredom, which could prevent you from being time-efficient. You don't have to start with the same set of chores every day, start with something different each new day, and take breaks in between.

10. Avoid Perfectionism

The last, but definitely not the least is that "Perfection is a state of mind and not an art". Perfection is very hard to achieve, but it's relatively easier to be organized. You need to realize your home can't always be perfect, but it could always be clean, organized, and comfy. The amount of time wasted on perfection can be spent on being organized and clean. The most important thing is "Organization" not "Perfection".

CONCLUSION

To crown it all, time management isn't a day job. It takes practice, practice to become a habit. Reward yourself, take breaks in between, make a realistic plan, stick to it, and don't procrastinate. In the end, you would realize you are a better time manager. If it worked for me, it could work for you too, but you need to know consistency is the key.

In the final analysis, time management as regards its definition means judiciously managing your time to produce efficiency and productivity. This book equips women with an understanding of techniques to be a successful working woman, and how-to-do lists can help you make your work simpler and easier.

It furthers habits working women should possess and finally making a distinction between urgency and importance. This book explains extensively, with examples of how to determine tasks that are intricate of productivity through the Urgent/Important Matrix. This is a book that repositions women's mentality about life and work balance, and how they can function in different capacities, without being lost or obsolete in one aspect.

I presume this masterpiece will help working mothers to prudently manage their time towards productivity and not expending on distractions and irrelevances.

I challenge all working women out there to read and digest exemplified contents and information in this book and would love to hear constructive criticism, comments and questions, feel free to chat me up on marienatoux83@gmail.com.

www.ingramcontent.com/pod-product-compliance
Lightning Source LLC
Chambersburg PA
CBHW021501210526
45463CB00002B/841